Dad and Wag

Shirleyann Costigan
Illustrations by Leanne Mebust

HAMPTON-BROWN

Wag ran off with Dad's cap.
That was funny.

Wag ran off with Dad's map.
That was funny, too.

Wag ran off with Dad's keys.
That was very funny.

Wag ran off with Dad's bag.
That was very funny, too.

Wag ran off with Dad!

That was <u>not</u> very funny!

That Wag!